MW00769106

CRADLE SONG

Copyright © 2009 by Stacey Lynn Brown

All rights reserved

Printed in the United States of America

Second Printing

No part of this book may be reproduced or used in any form or by any means without written permission from the publisher. This is a work of poetry; any resemblance to actual persons or events is purely coincidental.

ISBN 10: 0-9815010-5-2
ISBN 13: 978-0-9815010-5-5
LCCN: 2008936342

C&R Press
PO Box 4065
Chattanooga, TN 37405

www.crpress.org

Stacey Lynn Brown

CRADLE SONG
a poem

Stacey Lynn Brown

STACEY LYNN BROWN

For Vanesa —

who has many stories to tell
and many songs to sing. Your poem
tonight was amazing. I look forward
to having your book on my shelves
someday soon.

All good things,

5/14/12
NYC

CR

CRADLE SONG

Stacey Lynn Brown

for Gaither May Myrick
for my mother
and for Marley

CRADLE SONG

Stacey Lynn Brown

Index of First Lines

CRADLE SONG

Stacey Lynn Brown

CRADLE SONG

Foreword

Stacey Lynn Brown is a writer who knows that the raucous, honkeytonk instruments of Dixieland jazz were originally adapted from the military instruments played in the Civil War—the trumpet, fife, and drum going ahead of the young men walking into slaughter. Such ironic, articulate facts are dropped throughout the poems in *Cradle Song*, emblematic of the social and historical savvy of the poet and this poem. *Cradle Song* is a familial narrative, one that works at the knot of how black and white Americans have been, and always will be, *familially* entangled. In this particular family romance, we get the character of Gaither, the story-telling, tippling, profane and loving nanny, as known by the little white girl she cares for, our narrator.

The braided narratives of *Cradle Song* are satisfying because Brown understands the pungent paradoxical flavors of the South, the cotillions and the Klansmen, Rodney King, pot likker and the Evangelists, the generation whose "pride...kept them all writhing." To be a Southerner, says Brown, is to be forever draped in the past, with your feet or head exposed and cold. And these poems could only have been written by a Southern émigré, a runaway, someone both telling secrets and seeking perspective.

CRADLE SONG

The sequence, with its layered, interrupting voices, and episodic timejumping narrative, orbits through its stories, alternately inhabiting distanced social meditation and the fierce irrationalities of emotional attachment. "A sense of self in contrast to others/...is how Yankees endure," the narrator asserts; and then, a few poems later, "The first line of every racist joke/ is a quick look over each shoulder." Brown understands how many shades and flavors of illiteracy there might be.

"Prejudiced," we used to say, in a particular decade of American idiom, as if that was a simple and absolute thing, but *Cradle Song* is a *prejudicial* book, in the sense that its story is full of grief, resentment, humor, and love, full of points of view, as such a story must be to be true. It's a real accomplishment for this compelling book to find its way through such material without cliché, defendedness, or piety. *Cradle Song* is a resourceful book of poems, full of integrity, nerve, and insight. Like those Dixieland funerals—comical and tragic, full of tuba and clarinet—*Cradle Song* manages to be both an elegy and a celebration.

—*Tony Hoagland*

Stacey Lynn Brown

CRADLE SONG

Hush-a-bye, don't you cry, go to sleep my little baby,
When you wake, get some cake, and ride them pretty little horses,
Blacks and bays, dapples and grays, all them pretty little horses.
Way down yonder, down in the meadow, lies my poor little lambie,
Bees and butterflies peckin' out its eyes, poor little thing crying Mammy.

—Traditional Lullaby

CRADLE SONG

Stacey Lynn Brown

I.

When I was four, we drove to Nashville,
Grand Ole Opry-bound, and stopped
the night at a broken down motel
in Tennessee—shag walls,
mossy carpet, dank concrete—
and I remember standing in
the doorway as evening fell,
a busful of believers rattling their way
to the pool for a makeshift
baptism, the *Amens* and *Hear us, Lords*
ricocheting through the courtyard
as underwater lights glowed
the pool algae green.

They would come to him, the big
preacher man, and he'd lay
a palm across their foreheads, brace
them at the small of their backs.
They'd release themselves to him:
teethsucking the air before
falling back into salvation,
held under unstruggling and
splashing up anew all gasping
grace and sanctified glory
hallelujah til my mother shut the door
and made me watch tv.

My parents don't recall it,
but that's the way
memory works in the South—
the truth is always lying
in some field somewhere between
the bones of the fallen
and the weapons they reach for.

CRADLE SONG

II.

Down South, all it takes
to be a church are some stencils
and a van. And my childhood
was full of them:

The Episcopal litanies of Sunday school
exercises in genuflection,
the low country Southern Baptist pit
of hellfire and damnation

hemming us inside the tent
while just outside,
flies hoverbuzzed above
plattered chicken, slaw, and beans.

Prophets profiteering in spoken
tongues as the Charismatic
wailed and thrashed and shook
their Babel babble down.

In dirt-floored shacks, fevered
believers danced themselves
into a frenzy, coiling snakes like copper
bracelets dangling from their wrists,

spit-cracked lips and boot heel clog,
the bass line itself almost enough
to give you back your faith.
Grape juice in Dixie

cups, cardboard host, backwashed
wine, this grit who'd been told
to be still and learn
was never any closer to God

than when I stood at the back of that
whitewashed clapboard A.M.E. I could only
ever visit: The preacher pacing the worn
strip of rug, pleading, *Help us, Lord,*

teach us how to love,
sending testified ripples that washed
over heads nodding bobs
on the waves of his words:

choir rocking, feet stomping, peace
only to be found in the swing skirt of shimmy
and the big-bellied voices booming it holy
in the gospel of *move and know* sway.

CRADLE SONG

III.

If you would or could not do
for yourself, you hired a nanny
or wet nurse: cateyed Gaither
rolling in each day
to take up my bundled being
and soothe me, sustenance.

She raised me: balling my fists
to teach me to fight, shaming my hips
loose so I could shimmy, count cards,
ante up, winner takes all
dozen *yo mama's so uglies* on home.

All my childhood's most
important lessons, taught between
ducked out drags of Salems and Kools.
I answered only to her
name for me: *Big Legged Mama*
in servitude to her, gratefully.

IV.

Gaither memory #42:

*This one time, back when I was drinkin', I was sittin' up on the porch
and this old busy so and so come up to me and ask me could she have
a drink of my bag, and I says, "Have? Didn't nobody done let me
<u>have</u> this here bottle, why should I let you <u>have</u> any of it? Git yer own
damn bottle, you old so and so..."*
*And that ole lady commenced to hollerin' at me and fussin' and she come up
at me but I had my sister, see, what's got about a six inch blade,
so I got my sister out a my sock and started to cuttin' that ole busy up,
jus' hookin' it in, afore I realized I'd better git on out a there,
so I run over to a friend's what had a place where she was stayin' at
near there but she wouldn't open up the door for me, just opened it enough
for to see me through that chain, then shut it back again.*
*So I run on home and changed my clothes and then I went back to <u>that</u>
busy's house and did the same damn thing to her.*
Your daddy bailed me out a the jail that night, but he didn't know what for.
What happened to that first lady you cut up, Gate?
She didn't never walk again.

V.

Forgive me, Pumpkin, Gaither's true
daughter, for taking her from you
before the sun rose every day
and returning her, spent, at night.
I didn't know anyone could
love or need her more than I did,
those five days of your motherless week.

VI.

My mother's Gaither memory #29:

You and Amy were maybe three and five that year.
It was Christmas Eve, and we wanted to go to midnight church,
so we got Gaither to come and watch you. When we got home, it was late,
and when we turned on the living room lights, there was Gaither, passed out
and snoring up a storm beneath the Christmas tree. Your father went to wake her,
and when she came to, she sat up and sang, "Siiiiiiiuhlent Niiiiiiiite"
before passing right back out again. After that, we put a lock on the liquor cabinet
so she wouldn't have to go, you two loved her so.
How many times did you fire her, Mom?
Oh, I couldn't even count.

CRADLE SONG

VII.

Kristan clogged to *Rocky Top*
at her wedding, didn't want
her baby born a Yankee so took
a slow train south in the dusk
of her ninth month: Virginia
born in the squalling drawl
of *Mama*.

I left my accent in a gas station
in Kansas on the move out west.
Too much time spent
in front of audiences beaming back
sympathy for the slow wittedness
implicit in my speech:

I didn't catch what she was saying,
but didn't her words taste sweet?

Now it only ever comes out
when I'm back home, or drunk,
or just plain mad. Better watch
the combination of all three:
the knock-kneed grit rairin' up
skunk drunk, palms fisted
for the rain of blows to come.

Stacey Lynn Brown

VIII.

Sherman's march slithered through the South
with the alliteration he felt entitled to,
ku klux clinging like a kudzu curse,
like the carpetbaggers soon to come.

Laying over in Savannah, his commanders slept
in commandeered houses on the cobbled streets
(with the silver and women hidden just out of view)
while the infantry camped nearby, bedding

down across cemetery plots. Taking out their
knives, they carved their relief in the marble fonts,
scraping names, changing dates, the dead now dying
long before their births.

And then that third grade history book, its chapter
The War of Northern Aggression
so convincing in its righteousness
that my friend and I agreed

it was a good thing that we'd won or else
slaves would have never been freed.
How could we be the bad
guys when everyone I knew

was decent and kind, stirred slow
like sugar melting in sun tea?

IX.

Gaither's vacation postcard to her husband, #1:

Dear Moose,
I ain't never seen so much water.
And I can't even swim.

I never met the man, but my mother says
his back was like a Tennessee road map,
all scars and cratered gashes where Gaither
put the hurt on him.

        ❧

That trip was her first vacation
with us, the first time she'd seen
the ocean, the last time she'd ever eat
in public with our family.

At a little café in Alabama, she heard
what people had to say about her,
sitting at our table
like she belonged.

After that, she'd always cook
meals for herself at home.
My mother tried to tell her,
Just ignore them, Gaither, they're ignorant.

But white folks cannot fix by night
what they break in the light of day,
and it's a luxury of race to believe
that race is not an issue.

X.

Keeping us is what they called it,
someone else in charge, in possession, in lieu,
as if we were theirs to give—

(My father had a nanny.
His father had a leather pouch
and the shoes on his feet
when he came down from the foothills of north Georgia
to live with Aunt Lola in the city.

My mother had a back injury.
Her mother had a man to do her bidding,
a son who never left home, the Lord,
and a pride that left them all writhing.

Gaither was a natural choice.
She had leathered hands and woven braids
and an intolerance for tolerance.
She smelled like sweat and tobacco and linseed oil
and was given to us, was given us)

—as if we could be given back.

CRADLE SONG

XI.

Georgia boasts the largest outcrop
of granite in the world: bald
Stone Mountain long revered
by the Cherokee as holy,

and now upon its face, the carved
icons of our defeat: Jackson,
Davis, and Lee, horseback
and caped in their chivalry.

It took a crew of masons nearly sixty
years to finish, its scale so vast
nine men could shelter
in the nostril of a horse come rain.

Backdrop of my summers spent
picnicking on open fields
while rednecks circled its wide base
in stomper 4x4s.

Each night at dusk, the laser show
would beam its green technology
on the face of that monumental rock:
trapezoids and triangles pulsating to

jazz fusion grooves, crude cartoons:
The Devil Went Down to Georgia
clearly kicking young Johnny's ass,
Ray Charles and Willie Nelson swapping

Georgia on My Mind.
And in the finale, General Lee
would guide us again in fluorescent relief,
unsheathing his sword to lead his men

at a galloping gait
across battlefields laid to waste:
canons smoking, bodies slumped
in dying's contorted certainty.

And reckoning the cost
as he measured what was lost, he
broke his sword across his knee
in a motion of civility—

no treaties or humiliation,
no surrender under an old oak tree,
just this revisionary choice, a gift,
a balm, a necessary gesture

sure to assuage the Rebs on blankets
on the lawn, whooping the nobility of it all.

XII.

The first time I ever spit
the word *racist* at my father,
I was twelve, head full
of knowing better, heart sinking

with the realization I'd continue to have
that everything that I'd been told
was not necessarily so.

Slamming the door, I threw
myself down on my Laura Ashley
spread and cried like an adult
for the first time in my life.

In the years to come, my father and I
would vary little on that racist theme,
when it arose, and now it hovers
close enough to harm the man I love:
British, Irish, Sicilian, Lebanese,
no other Others bothered him,
just this gelatinous mix
of dark and light, Us
and the most nefarious
of Them all.

It wouldn't be fair to blame my dad
for what's right or wrong or old.

Contempt doesn't work, as it implies

Stacey Lynn Brown

disrespect I don't otherwise feel.
And I'm not trying to shame
or indict. It's just

It's just what, Big Legs?

To be a Southerner is to feel yourself
forever draped in the mantle of the past,
to pull at the corners of that threadbare
quilt and know its incongruity, the feet
or head always left bare, exposed
to the elemental cold.

Stacey Lynn Brown

disrespect I don't otherwise feel.
And I'm not trying to shame
or indict. It's just

It's just what, Big Legs?

To be a Southerner is to feel yourself
forever draped in the mantle of the past,
to pull at the corners of that threadbare
quilt and know its incongruity, the feet
or head always left bare, exposed
to the elemental cold.

33

XIII.

Southern language lesson #1:

When insulting or slandering a person,
bless them before and after, as in
That Evelyn, bless her heart, she's got
quite a nasty drinking habit, the poor dear.

In the South, it's considered ungracious to speak
ill of the living or dead,
which is why so much
of our conversation
seems to focus on the weather, and food.

The first line of every racist joke
is a quick look over each shoulder.

And on the scales of Southern contempt, no one
falls below White Trash,
that condition without excuse.

XIV.

Most nights that she'd keep us,
Gaither staged a fight
between my two balled fists:
cinching her fingers round
the base of my hands, she made

Big Legs on the right
roll sets on lefty *Mama.*
And when my mother
came home, I hid from her
my bruised knuckles and wrung-red wrists.

Other nights, rap jack,
the game of switches
set against bare legs
with the loser the first one to cry.

It's how I learned to hold it in,
to take more pain than I could bear,
and that winning
is a relative idea.

CRADLE SONG

XV.

Forgive her, Pumpkin, Gaither's true
daughter, for her first time driving, afternoon, accident,
so unsure of the gas, the brake, and the clutch, just
the squealing tire smoke and the aching, dull thud
as you crumpled into the past. I didn't know
anyone could love or need me more
than she did, every day of her daughterless weeks.

XVI.

3 a.m. feedings were bottled affairs,
with my mother asleep and Gaither
sleeping it off, so my father would
rock me in the wicker chair, formula
for me, Red Ripple for him, softly
singing *You are my special angel*
sent from heaven above while we studied
each other with drowsying eyes
there in the nightlight glow.

XVII.

Family legend #27:

The summer of my second birthday,
we took a trip to the panhandled Gulf—
yellow cottage, gritty floors, those
villainous sand fleas—and the whole
family was watching as my sister and I
rolled a ball on the beach between us.

And when she refused to roll it
back to me, I curled up my fist,
set my hand on my hip,
and gave up my first full sentence:

Give me the damn ball, Amy.
Shock. Silence. Then my father
asked, *Where on earth'd*
she learn language like that?
And Gaither, laughing like
the devil's own:
Hell if I know, Mister Bob.

XVIII.

At least once a month, we'd load up in Big Bertha,
the station wagon my father bought
the year that I was born, and squabble the first
few miles out of town, vying for backseat space.

Up I-85, we'd stop halfway
for sausage biscuits and sweet iced tea,
then settle back to watch the scenery:
red clay fields, bristled crops, ribboned oaks.

At Bern Circle, feral cats would flee
the crunching of Bertha's tires, my grandmother
bursting through the back-flung door
in a cloud of talcum and cold cream, bellowing,

Herrrrrrr-burt! They're heah! as she swept us up
into her arms. Grandfather loping out to pull me close
against his chest, Uncle walking crookedly from his room
of towering *Playboys* and stashed cash.

Once dinner was finished, they'd all gather round
the upright piano as my grandmother banged
her sweet ragtime will and as a group once more they became
The Rice Family Gospel Singers:

On air over fifty years,
radio and television,
gospel of chitlin circuits
and tented revival revues.

Escaping, my mother had turned the quartet
into a trio years back,
but when she came home, she blended it in
as if she had never left:

CRADLE SONG

In The Sweet By and By,
How Great Thou Art,
and *Home Sweet Home*
were how I learned to sing,

sliding the scales til I found harmony
and the place I could hold with them,
watching my mother (to learn how to) fake
belonging in my own family.

XIX.

When I was three, we were eating dinner
at Lester Maddox's chicken shack,
the man himself slow-wheeling through the crowd
like breeze from a ceiling fan.

I'd just learned how to make farting noises
with my hand inside my armpit
and proudly called out, *Hey, Dad, look at me*
as I flapped and squawked earnestly.

My mortified mother hissed *Hush* at me
as Lester Maddox approached, and scooping me up
he held me high like a trophy above his head:
Now this is a great kid!

The grinning grit's unwitting coronation
by a Klansman who dropped his hood.

XX.

Southern cooking lesson #1:

Lack of soul does not preclude white men
from going hungry: recipes handed across
lines of poverty first, then race—
economic in nature, like war.

Memo to the carpetbaggers, proudly flouring
chicken in their Fry Daddys:
The greens are not the most
desirable, just discarded

once the turnips had been picked.
Fatback makes all the difference.
Pot likker is water seasoned up to quell
a belly still rumbling.

Making use of what remained
in fields and on killing floors,
just as what was left over after the war
remained for survival's sake:

A sense of self in contrast to others
is necessary, is how *Yankees* endure.

XXI.

Growing up, I knew more about football
than ballet or Barbie dolls, pigskin
in the South second only to God,
and only then on the Sabbath day.

I'd edge into pickup games with the boys
and they'd take me in—*y'all get the girl*—
but made me run wide, sweeping hooks

that kept me clear out of the way
til the day Jackson wrenched his rotator cuff
and they let me try quarterback.

I spread my fingers through the laces
the way my dad had taught me to
and sent it spiraling clean and long
into Kenneth's outstretched arms.

From then on, I was all-time
boy: fists full of hair, sunken teeth,
fractured bones, their brawling bodies

dogpiling me down
and always a quick, anonymous squeeze
where one day my breasts would be.

XXII.

My father's nanny, James Anna Swain,
kept us when Gaither couldn't be found
or couldn't be sobered up.

In her house in Decatur, my sister and I
would fix Jiffy Pop on the hot stovetop
and walk carefully room to room,

avoiding the grill of the metal furnace
she'd fallen through years ago,
scarring her leg in third degree burns

that stole all the color from her skin:
swath of pink we could claim as kin.
She braided our hair into rows like her own

and taught us how to sew, saying,
I reckon it's only ever good to know
how to darn socks for a man.

Early lesson from the vault
of how to keep and please.

XXIII.

My Gaither memory #133:

I was probably 11 or 12,
leaning back on my bed, all
dreamy-eyed, listening to
Sometimes When We Touch,
or *Endless Love,* and Gaither
strode through, took one look
at me, and over her shoulder,
on her way out the door: *Stop thinkin'*
about them boys, Big Legs.
They ain't nuthin'
but no damn good.

CRADLE SONG

XXIV.

Gaither-kept night #912:

Supper was rutabagas
and blackeyed peas, half dollar
biscuits and buttermilk.

I'd just started taking
guitar lessons
down at the music store

and hated it, the eight-note scales
sounding nothing like
the music I wanted to make,

his thick fingers pressing
down on mine
to force me to strum the chords true.

Hunched over the cherrywood
frame, I painfully fretted
the songlist he'd prescribed:

*Red River Valley, Yellow Rose
of Texas, Hang Down
Your Head, Tom Dooley.*

But I laid it down once and for all
when Gaither harrumphed
from across the room:

*Don't mean nuthin' til you can play
this,* she said, as Quincy thumped
Sanford and Son.

Stacey Lynn Brown

XXV.

At nine, I found myself mighty
curious about those cigarettes
Gaither smoked.

This was years before I'd get hellbent
on trying to make her quit,
finding the packs she'd hidden from me
and flushing them down the john,

years before Christmas Eve meant
bringing cartons and cash to her place.

Back then, all I knew
was that I loved her husky laugh,
the way the stubbed out duck behind her ear
settled her nerves from can to can't.

I asked her for one, and she studied me
hard, then thumped it stiff out the pack.

I guess she thought I'd take one drag
and fall coughing and green to the ground,
but I took that Kool between my lips—her style—

and smoked that so and so all the way down
to the filter while she just laughed
and clucked her tongue at me.

You promised you wouldn't never tell, Big Legs.
I know, Gaither May. I know.

XXVI.

One Christmas, I got an air rifle
in a long cardboard box, and I learned
to close one eye to balance
the lollipop sights, how to hold
my breath steady and then exhale
the tinny *pap* of compressed air.
My father taught me to love
the pinwheel bullseye of marksmanship,
but my godfather cop taught me

draw only to kill, how to click back
the hammer fast and first.
Down at the precinct firing
range, we'd motor black
silhouetted bad guys
back and forth to tally our scores:
yellow goggles filtering shattered
light, ears plugged against the report,
I ripped star-shaped holes
in manila flesh, bracing
against kickback.

I shot .357s, automatics, revolvers,
the black smoke barrel of his .45
regulation in the palm of my hand.
I learned to steady the weight, leveled
line from my chin, the quick draw
from waist, shoulder holster, or boot.

In all that time, I never asked
how many people he had killed.
Every story he told me ended
hammer cocked and chamber loaded against
the temple of the criminal.

48

Stacey Lynn Brown

In pool halls and bars
since then, I've looked down
the other end of revolvers,
felt the snubnose muzzle, sliding slick

in the divot in between my eyes.
A sudden crack, the powder clouds,
bodies crumpling like coats
on the floor.

And when I worked late
at the nightclub and had to carry
a .38, the steel in leather felt right
against my ribs. Still, I dream

the same single shot. Some nights,
I know how the hollow point
explodes my skull into darkness.

CRADLE SONG

XXVII.

My grandfather who, in his day, had been tyrant, holy,
keeper of the gothic ornaments of religion, strict, penitent,
and unlistening, obstinate slammer of doors and disavowing
thief of family, was, in the end, reduced in that diapering
inevitability to velcro shoes and sweatshirts with his name
sewn in the collar.

Through the halls of the hollerers he ambled his walker, navigating
the squeaky labyrinth of disease, despair, and dementia, down
to the Medicare wing, his picture on the door to guide him
to the right bed beside an endless stream of roommates reaching
their ends, their messy living and dying scrubbed down,
then freshly sheeted.

My grandfather who, in his day, painted landscapes so beautiful
I wanted to live inside them, sang baritone and bass gospel on
revival chitlin circuits, taught classes in foot care for sciatic-sore
millworkers, and bagged groceries at the Bi-Lo after car and child
collided, was, in the end, only able to remember fits and starts
of *Amazing Grace.*

Through four nursing homes he listed aimlessly, building model
Fords from popsicle sticks, singing fragments of redemption songs,
his vast immobility childing him small and sunken like the furthest
flung stone against a glass house of dying, lobbed up and heavied
back down again to the room where I would sit, holding his absence,
his paper-thin hand.

XXVIII.

When New Orleans musicians
inherited instruments

left over from the Civil War,
Dixieland Jazz was born.

Trumpet, fife, snare and tom
were witnesses, called to testify.

And when Deacon Lunchbox died,
a thousand mourners turned out to grieve

the poet who worked construction by day
and gave readings in a bra, with chainsaw.

From the Austin Avenue Buffet, the band
slow dragged *Just A Closer Walk With Thee*

all the way up to Oakland Cemetery
before swinging into *Didn't He Ramble?*

back home to the Yacht Club. Dirge
for all the poems he left

unpunctuated, unsung.

XXIX.

Whenever Gaither got fired, Juanita
stepped in, her opposite in every way—
plump and maternal and young where Gaither
was flint and gristle and wire.
My love for her felt treacherous.
Like the day they met, on accident:
Gaither coming down off a drunk
and showing up at our house, convinced,
Juanita dusting my parents' bedroom, all shock
and sweet surprise. I knew better when I saw
Gaither go for her sock, saw, for the first time,
the glint of steel in her eyes that matched her blade. I knew
it was time to get her out of the house, so we went
for a walk. It was my first lie to her:
You don't love that so and so, do you?

XXX.

Gaither memory #49:

This one time, I was stayin' up at them high rised apartments
over by Georgia Baptist, and we was all the way up on the fifth
floor, Sister's girl and me, and one day when she come home
from the bus, some nogoodnik seen her walkin' and started to
followin' her, all a the way up the stairs and on down the hall,
and when she was half a the way in the door, he come up from behind
and they commenced to tusslin' and he was tryin' to...
well, he weren't up to no good...
and I was in the kitchen, fryin' in the pan, and I heard her commence to
hollerin' "Auntie Gate, Auntie Gate" like she done rung up the dead,
so I run in there and saw what he was fixin' to do to that child
and I brung that skillet in and swung it upside his head what with
everything I got til it near bout took his fool head off,
and the grease was still hot and he was hollerin' at me and cussin'
but I kept on a swingin' til I got him good and buckled up
over by them windows, and then I hit him one last time and pushed
his sad self on out.
Out of a five story window? What happened to him, Gate?
I don't reckon that's none of my concern.

CRADLE SONG

XXXI.

When the jury reached a verdict
on the Rodney King assault,
I was researching at Morehouse College,
nose deep in Grier and Cobb.

Stepping out into the sunlight,
the campus throbbed an angry pulse
as bodies tumbled out of buildings,
currented in their rage:

Cars rocking, bricks in flight, and as I made
my way to the Marta station, I asked
the nearest person what
was happening, what was wrong.

What's wrong is you'd better get
your white ass outta here, which I did,
but not before their rocks and bottles
found their mark on me.

I rode with one hand pressed against
my bloody crown, but understood
since it's true what they say, since on the surface,
we *do* all look the same.

XXXII.

At the Flannery O'Connor
homestead there's nothing left
of the godly writer's work
but these peacocks roosting
in trees at dusk, screaming
like children at the dark.

XXXIII.

When it came time, I would leave the South,
trailing a U-Haul

behind my mother's Cadillac
and driving west til the land ran out.

There's something unnamable
at the point where all you see

is water ahead and what you've left
behind, your shadow so soon

to catch up with you
as the sun sinks finally down.

XXXIV.

In Springfield, Oregon, I hung the state
of Georgia flag above my bed,
remembering what my father said
just before I left:

If you can't sleep
with red clay beneath your feet,
at least you can see
the Stars and Bars above.

A collector's item now, unfurled it meant
making *please understand me* love
to men who never stood a chance
beneath its long-dead, distant light.

XXXV.

When I missed the South the most, I'd take
to dating one of its sons: gentlemen
callers who held the door
with tapered fingers or rough
field hands. What I was looking
for was never to be found
in them, just something like it,
the way a lake can bring to mind
but never *be* the sea.

XXXVI.

Perspective takes distance, I would learn,
but every summer cycled me home
to magnolias in cicada-heavy nights
and the room I had as a child,
flowered paper peeling back,
Humpty Dumpty peeking through,
my old brass bed pressed like an ear
against a wall that never kept secrets.

Terminus. Marthasville.
The town my father grew up in
is an Epcot exhibit of Long Ago:
trolley cars and friendly strangers
in seersucker suits and brimmed straw hats.

The town I grew up in
a stenciled sketch of what was
coming, what we refused to see,

like those medical textbooks
with transparent overlays
that teach what lies beneath:
skin, muscles, nerves, and blood
striating in layers above caged bone, this city
built on its own remains.

The tour guide narrating The Battle
of Atlanta speaks in a thick chowder brogue,
and as children, we are taught
that when we shudder from the inside out with a chill,
it's Yankees walking over our graves.

XXXVII.

Phone call from my mother, 1996:

Well, it was already an honor just to be named
on the Court of The Gracious Ladies.
I never expected to win. I mean, it's such a prestigious award,
coming from the oldest society in the South
dedicated to the good and charitable works
of women who volunteer.

But the funniest thing was what happened the night
of the ceremony in Columbus. There we were, in our most
elegant gowns, escorted by Marines in dress blues.
And just as I was walking through the silver-sabered arch,
a man climbed up the scaffolding
and mooned us from the catwalk.

Can you imagine? I'd just been crowned
The Most Gracious Lady in Georgia,
and everyone was looking to see how I would act.
Really, it was all I could do not to swoon on the spot,
but I just smiled and gave a little curtsey, which I thought
was the gracious thing to do.

Wow. Those are some pretty big shoes to fill, Mom.
They're pumps, darling. They're pumps.

XXXVIII.

Sepia sister of a different kind, unseen you, your absence
was palpable. You should have moved six feet, one inch,
three yards to the left, the right, into view, back into sight,
you should have stayed inside, should have lived on
into that night and every one to come. You could have
given her so much, should have gone to school, sharpened
pencils, new lunchbox, pigtails and Mary Janes.

But those are my details. In reality, you would have been
wearing my sister's old clothes, *outgrown but not worn out,*
my mother would have said, you should have had the first
crush, first kiss, first love, first loss instead of absence
and nothing and nothing again.

You deserved so much more than her
I made her and I reckon I can make me another,
so much more than whatever words the preacher summoned
as he rained earth down on

you still deserve so much more, you should have lived
and you, I know, there is no doubt, you
would have hated me.

CRADLE SONG

IXL.

Gaither Memory, The Last:

Dementia meant a slow unraveling, faces
moving backwards, a siphoned creep:
the digits of our number lost
as the fickle past stayed passed.

And so we searched: landlords, kinfolk,
tracking her down at an eldercare home,
five deep on cots per room.
And when I walked in, she scowled at me,

glaring up with just one good eye:
Where the hell you been, Big Legs?

(We'd missed it all—the darkening vision,
her cataract eye, the labcoated doctors
and their Medi-caring ways, removing
what could have been saved. And instead

of a fake, she had in its place
a cat's eye marble, rolling round aimlessly.)

She gave me a tour, ignoring the leers
from the pot-bellied men playing rounds of bid whist
in a kitchen that reeked of the burned
before sitting on the porch for a smoke.

I left her that day with money and Kools
and the promise that I'd be back soon.
But three days later, we got a call
from the woman who ran the place

saying Gaither had just up and left,
walked out without a word,
and could we please come and collect
the things she left behind?

In the years since then, I've looked for her
in phone books, hospitals, and jails,
the blocked text of obituaries
before stopping my search, the desire

to know weighing less than the fear
of what I might find out. Maybe
it's true what my mother says—
that I'm being protected, that I'm not meant

to know what became of her. Maybe.
Still, the child she kept sits waiting in that house,
hoping she'll find her way back somehow
and show up one day, convinced.

CRADLE SONG

XL.

Gaither Memory, Every Working Day:

Me in play clothes, her masquerading
as a maid: no short black skirt and feather
duster but a stiff brown dress with white
stitched pockets where she kept tissues
and half-smoked ducks.

Perched on top of the white deep
freezer next to the ironing board,
I kept her company while she did
chores: dousing water from an old
Coke bottle on badly wrinkled shirts,

spitting to check the iron's flat
metal heat, mating socks and snapping
sheets. The best part of her day
was my worst: changing back into
her street clothes, hanging up

the uniform, Bony Maroni
all angles and knees in our castoff
hand-me-downs. I'd walk her
to the street to wait
for the bus that carried her home

two transfers and three hours later,
and stand waving goodbye
in the black diesel fumes
while my mother called me in to eat
the supper left warming on the stove.

Stacey Lynn Brown

Epilogue

1.

Pregnancy means revisiting your own—
past, childhood, mother. You vow:
things you will do differently, people
you won't become.

Halfway through my mine, my mother calls:
*You know, with my back injury, I didn't get to hold you
until you were nine months old.*

I think about this every day
I am pregnant, every day
after my daughter is born.

My mother missed more
than what she never had,
the even weight of this child
on my chest, skin to skin, breath to breath.
Her presence is so much more
than the lack of absence, the way *mothering*

moves with its own pulse
beyond what is physical.

2.

When she visits, we lie on my bed
while I nurse my child. *I never felt that,
don't even know how it feels.*
Her milk never let down. And I think,
as always, of Gaither, imagine

my pale face pressed against her, my eyes
brimming over the curve of her skin.
She would love this child, the way
I still love Pumpkin, half-sister, unseen.

3.

In the nightlight glow, I rock
my daughter, piece together a lullaby
from the patchwork of the past—

borrowing the melody
of *You Are My Special Angel*, I add
melancholia for the let-down, the unsuckled,
and the lost, and a whiskey-soaked
blues for the undead. I kiss
her forehead, whisper soft

Hey, Big Legs, where you been?

Stacey Lynn Brown

CRADLE SONG

Grateful acknowledgement is made to the editors of the following publications where some of these poems appeared:

Natural Bridge: "Lack of soul does not preclude white men"
"When it came time, I would leave the South"
"In Springfield, Oregon, I hung the state"

Sou'wester: "If you would or could not do/for yourself"
"Forgive me, Pumpkin, Gaither's true"
"Me in play clothes, her masquerading"
Epilogue

Anti-: "Kristan clogged to *Rocky Top*"
"Growing up, I knew more about football"

Audio and text versions of several of these poems are available online at *From the Fishouse: An Audio Archive of Emerging Poets* (www.fishousepoems. org). "Down South, all it takes/to be a church" will be included in the anthology *From the Fishouse: An Anthology of Poems that Sing, Rhyme, Resound, Syncopate, Alliterate, and Just Plain Sound Great*, forthcoming in 2009.

"When I was four, we drove to Nashville," "Down South, all it takes" and "My grandfather, who, in his day, had been tyrant" were winners in the 14th Annual Poetry Center of Chicago Juried Reading Series and appear in an anthology by dancing girl press.

I am immensely grateful to the good people at C&R Press, Ryan G. Van Cleave, Chad Prevost, and James Iredell, for their faith in me and for bringing this book into the light. I am also indebted to Tony Hoagland for originally selecting this manuscript and to John McCracken, Esq., for helping me to reclaim it.

I'd like to thank my teachers, Janella Brand, W.N. Herbert, Peter Parker, Frank Manley, Judson Mitcham, Ferrol Sams, Garrett Hongo, and T.R. Hummer, with special thanks to Dorianne Laux for her continued

friendship and support. My friends, Frank and Julie Houston, Eddy
Nahmias, Cheryl Kopec Nahmias, Matt Banks, Adam and Naomi Hintz,
Brian Reardon, Mike Bono, Kristan Adams, Jim Knoer, Jade, and Steven
Rumbelow. My family, especially my parents, my sister Amy, Morgan and
Sydney, Ruth Plaster Noble, Herbert Rice, Cecil Chatham, Bud and Leesa
Sosebee, Emily Nuckolls, and Martha Jeanne Darnes. I am grateful for my
Oregon family, Teresa Brooks-Hernandez, Hugo Hernandez, Alexandra
Smith, Tommy Mang, Ken Goldberg, Fiona McAuliffe, Hazel Redmon,
Flint Livingston-Confer, and Isabelle Confer, and for the creative Atlanta
of a certain time: the Mudd Shack, FLAP, Benjamin and Opal Foxx, DQE,
Deacon Lunchbox, Follow for Now, and The Jody Grind.

Many thanks to the writers who read and vouched for my book, both on
the back cover and elsewhere, and to the poets and writers who inspire
me, advise me, and have graced my life with their work: Oliver de la Paz,
Sean Singer, Paul Guest, Lyrae Van Clief-Stefanon, Quraysh Ali Lansana,
Sherwin Bitsui, Ruth Ellen Kocher, Kristian Bush, Tracy Daugherty, Ehud
Havazelet, Joe Millar, Kyle Minor, and Ilya Kaminsky. An immeasurable
debt is owed to Allison Joseph and Jon Tribble, friends, poets, editors,
advisors, and confidants.

Thanks to my colleagues, Geoff Schmidt, Allison Funk, and Valerie Vogrin,
and to Matt O'Donnell and the wonderful work he does at the Fishouse.
Thanks to Southern Oregon University and Elizabeth Udall for The
Walden Residency Fellowship and to Michael Bohrer-Clancy and his family
for giving me time and space to write. And finally, heartfelt thanks to my
oldest and closest poet friend, Brian Turner, whose continued faith—and
faith in me—sustains.

And to my own family—my amazing husband Adrian and the light of our
world, Marley—who have taught me more about love and being loved than I
ever could have known and who are always a chorus of comfort and joy:
thank you.

Stacey Lynn Brown

CRADLE SONG